A bright kitchen to be proud of!

Kitchen

Tea cozy and Place mats
Instructions on page 2

TEA COZY AND PLACE MATS

Kitchen

PICTURE ON P.1

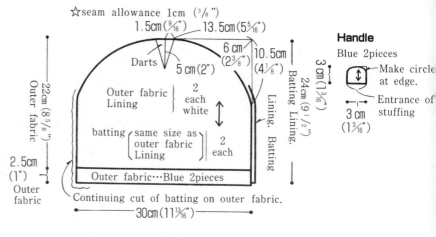

☆seam allowance 1cm (³/₈")

1.5cm (⁹/₁₆")   13.5cm (5⁵/₁₆")

Handle

Blue 2pieces

— Make circle at edge.

3cm (1³/₁₆") — Entrance of stuffing

3cm (1³/₁₆")

6cm (2³/₈")   10.5cm (4¹/₈")

Darts   5cm (2")

Outer fabric
Lining

2 each white

batting {same size as outer fabric, Lining}

2 each

Lining. Batting

24cm (9¹/₂") Batting Lining

22cm (8⁵/₈") Outer fabric

2.5cm (1") Outer fabric

Outer fabric···Blue 2pieces

Continuing cut of batting on outer fabric.

30cm (11¹³/₁₆")

〈Tea cozy〉

Materials

- White cotton 64cm×50cm (25³/₁₆"×19¹¹/₁₆")
- Blue cotton 37cm ×10cm (14⁹/₁₆"× 4")
- Batting   64cm ×55cm (25³/₁₆"× 21⁵/₈")
- Polyester stuffing
- #25 blue embroidery floss

Finished size : Depth 24.5cm (9⁵/₈")

⑧ Sew with right sides together, turn right side and add stuffing, blindstitch entrance of stuffing.

Handle

⑨ Sew tight.

③ Sew darts.

④ After making darts layer batting with other fabric and sew with right side together.

⑤ Layer batting with lining and sew same as outer fabric.

② Layer batting with outer fabric and embroider.

Tea time morning tea afternoon tea

① Sew right sides together, white and Blue.

14cm (5¹/₂")

Opening for turning

⑦ Turn right side and blindstitch opening.

⑥ With right sides together, outer fabric and lining, sew front and back sides leaving opening notch.

〈Place Mats〉

Materials (for 1)

- Blue cotton 88cm×32cm (34⁵/₈"×12⁵/₈")
- White cotton 9cm (3¹/₂") square
- Batting 44cm×32cm (17⁵/₁₆"× 12⁵/₈")
- #25 Blue embroidery floss

Finished size 42cm×30cm (16¹/₂"×11¹³/₁₆")

☆seam allowance is 1cm (³/₈")

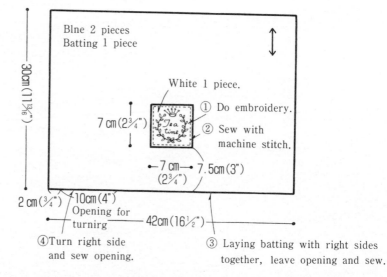

Blne 2 pieces
Batting 1 piece

White 1 piece.

① Do embroidery.

② Sew with machine stitch.

Tea time

7cm (2³/₄")

7cm (2³/₄")   7.5cm (3")

30cm (11¹³/₁₆")

2cm (³/₄") 10cm (4") Opening for turning

42cm (16¹/₂")

④Turn right side and sew opening.

③ Laying batting with right sides together, leave opening and sew.

⟨Tea cozy⟩

Actual size

☆Use 2 strands and satin stitch unless indicated other wise.

Outline stitch

Teatime

Back stitch

morning tea afternoon tea

⟨Place Mats⟩

Outline stitch

Tea time

Back stitch

Outline stitch

Continued from page 14
Actual size

☆Use 2 strands

Macrame stitch

Outline stitch

Chain stitch

Long and short stitch

Outline stitch

Satin stitch

Straight stitch

Center

Satin stitch

Satin stitch

Center

Kitchen

Table cloth

Instructions on page 6

Table cloth

Kitchen

PICTURE ON P.4

Materials

· Offwhite soft denim 112cm(44") square
· Moss green shirting fabric 48cm ×124cm
$$(18\,^7/_8\text{"}\times 48\,^{13}/_{16}\text{"})$$
· #25 embroidery floss dark greenish brown,
light greenish brown, dark old rose, light old rose,

Finished size : 120cm(47 1/4") square

Actual size

☆4 strands for
outline stitch

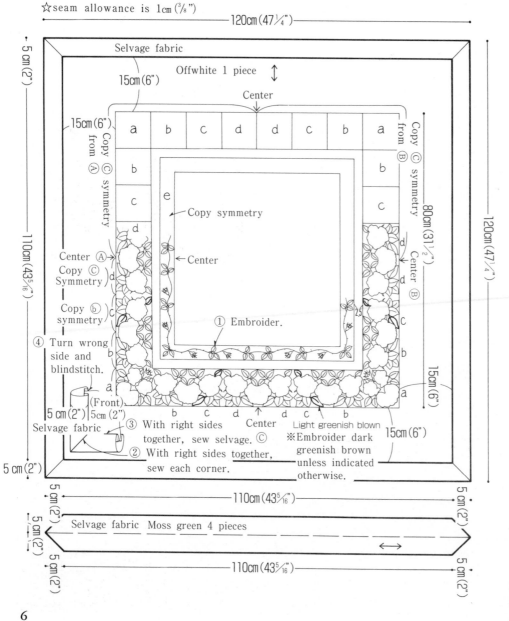

☆seam allowance is 1cm(³/₈")

120cm(47¼")

Selvage fabric

Offwhite 1 piece

15cm(6")

Center

15cm(6")

15cm(6")

| a | b | c | d | d | c | b | a |

Copy ⓒ from ⓐ

Copy ⓒ symmetry from Ⓑ

Copy ⓒ symmetry

b | b

c | c

80cm(31½")

Center Ⓐ
Copy ⓒ
Symmetry

d | d

Copy ⓑ symmetry c | Center Ⓑ

d | d

e → Copy symmetry

← Center

① Embroider.

④ Turn wrong side and blindstitch.

25

c | c

b | b

a | a

(Front)

5 cm(2") | 5cm(2")

15cm(6")

Selvage fabric

③ With right sides together, sew selvage. ⓒ

b c d Center d c b

15cm(6")

② With right sides together, sew each corner.

Light greenish blown

※Embroider dark greenish brown unless indicated otherwise.

120cm(47¼")

5 cm(2")

5 cm(2")

110cm(43⁵/₁₆")

5 cm(2")

110cm(43⁵/₁₆")

5 cm(2")

5 cm(2")

5 cm(2")

5 cm(2")

Selvage fabric Moss green 4 pieces

5 cm(2")

110cm(43⁵/₁₆")

5 cm(2")

← Center

e

Dark old rose

Dark greenish brown

Match wi
● P7 mar

#25 embroidery floss, use 3 strands and backstitch
  unless indicated otherwise

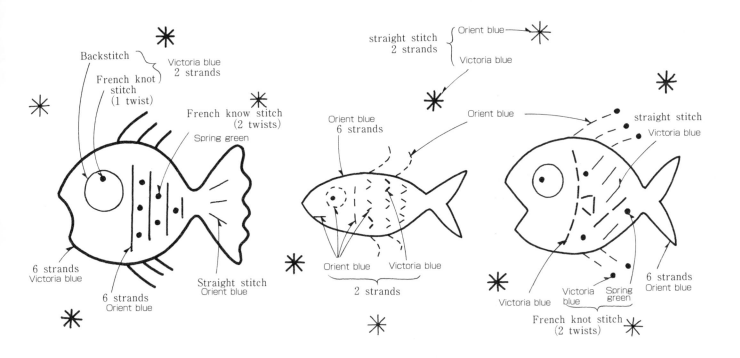

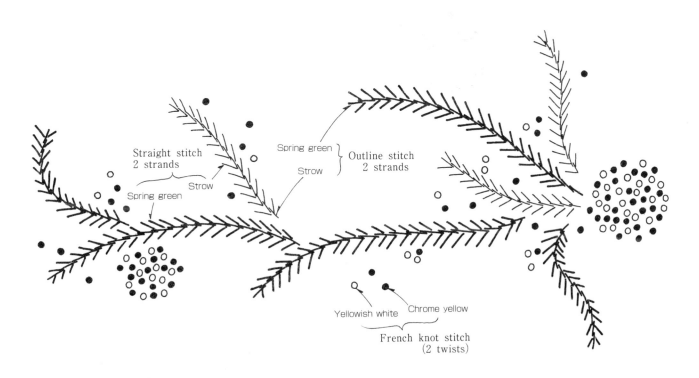

Kitchen

Pot holder (round shape, mitten shape)
Toaster cover, Towel stacker

Pot holder, Toaster cover ⋯ Instructions on page 14
Towel stacker ⋯ Instructions on page 55

Toaster cover and Pot holder
Kitchen

PICTURE ON P.12

⟨Toaster cover⟩
Materials
· Sky blue shirting fabric 82cm ×62cm
$(32^1/_4 " \times 24^7/_{16}")$
· #25 embroidery floss   olive green, blue,
old rose, Pale bluish purple
Finished size 39cm×60cm $(15^3/_8" \times 23^5/_8")$

Design on page 58

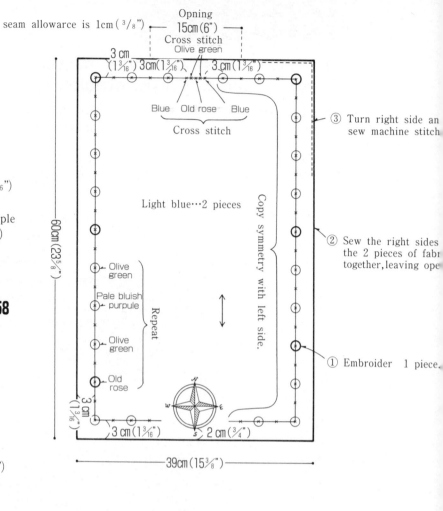

seam allowarce is 1cm ($^3/_8$")

Opning
15cm (6")
Cross stitch
Olive green

3 cm
$(1^3/_{16}")$ 3cm($1^3/_{16}"$) 3 cm($1^3/_{16}"$)

Blue Old rose Blue
Cross stitch

③ Turn right side an
sew machine stitch

Light blue···2 pieces

Copy symmetry with left side.

② Sew the right sides
the 2 pieces of fabr
together, leaving ope

Olive green

Pale bluish purple

Repeat

Olive green

Old rose

① Embroider 1 piece.

60cm (23$^5/_8$")

3 cm($1^3/_{16}"$)

3 cm ($1^3/_{16}"$)   2 cm ($^3/_4$")

39cm ($15^3/_8$")

⟨Pot holder (Round shape)⟩
Materials
· Blue cotton ···47cm $(18^1/_2")$ square
· Offwhite cotton···33cm×19cm $(13" \times 7^1/_2")$
· Offwhite quilt thread
· Batting 19cm $(7^1/_2")$ square
· #25 embroidery floss dark blue
Finished size : 19cm $(7^1/_2")$ diameter

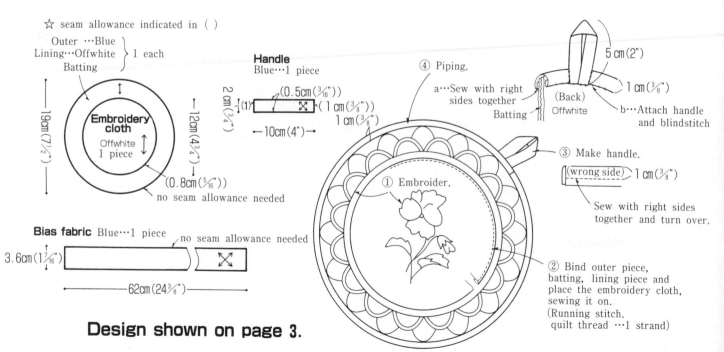

☆ seam allowance indicated in ( )

Outer ···Blue
Lining···Offwhite } 1 each
Batting

Embroidery cloth
Offwhite 1 piece

19cm (7$^1/_2$")

12cm (4$^3/_4$")

no seam allowance needed
$(0.8cm(^5/_{16}"))$

Handle
Blue···1 piece
2 cm($^3/_4$")(1) $(0.5cm(^3/_{16}"))$ (1 cm ($^3/_8$"))
1 cm ($^3/_8$")
←10cm(4")→

④ Piping.
a···Sew with right sides together
Batting

5 cm (2")
(Back)
Offwhite
b···Attach handle and blindstitch
1 cm ($^3/_8$")

① Embroider.

③ Make handle.
(wrong side) 1 cm ($^3/_8$")
Sew with right sides together and turn over.

② Bind outer piece,
batting, lining piece and
place the embroidery cloth,
sewing it on.
(Running stitch.
quilt thread ···1 strand)

Bias fabric Blue···1 piece
no seam allowance needed
3.6cm($1^7/_{16}$")
←————62cm(24$^3/_8$")————→

Design shown on page 3.

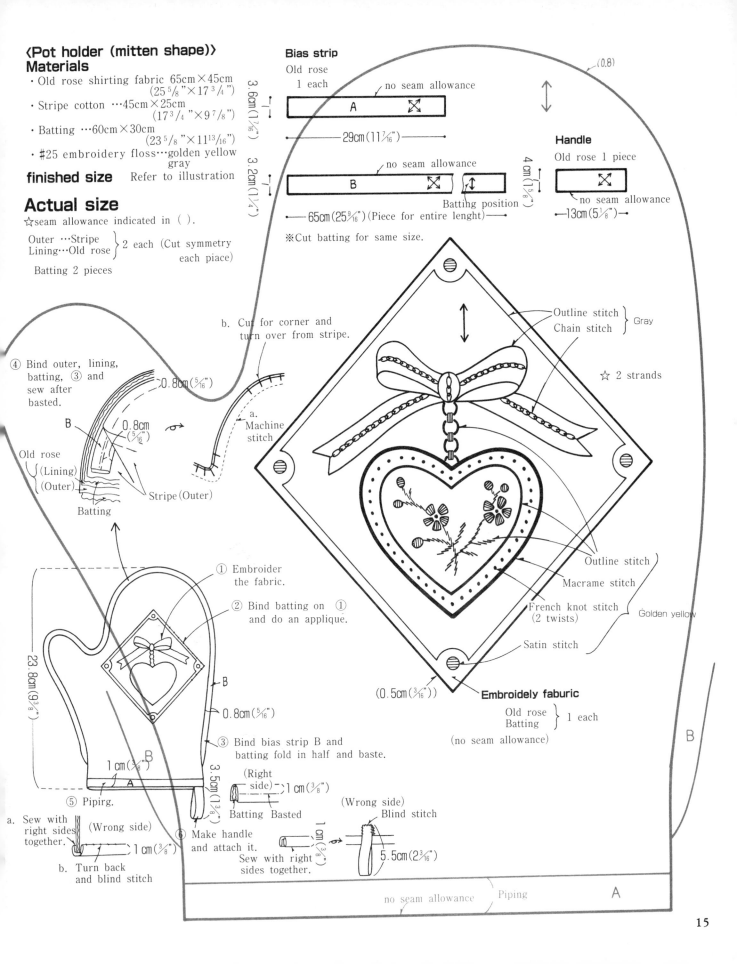

⟨Pot holder (mitten shape)⟩
Materials

· Old rose shirting fabric 65cm×45cm
   (25⅝"×17¾")
· Stripe cotton ···45cm×25cm
   (17¾"×9⅞")
· Batting ···60cm×30cm
   (23⅝"×11¹³⁄₁₆")
· #25 embroidery floss···golden yellow
   gray

finished size   Refer to illustration

Actual size

☆seam allowance indicated in ( ).

Outer ···Stripe
Lining···Old rose } 2 each (Cut symmetry each piace)

Batting 2 pieces

Bias strip
Old rose
1 each   no seam allowance

A ⊠

3.6cm(1⁷⁄₁₆)
── 29cm(11⁷⁄₁₆") ──

no seam allowance

B ⊠   ⇕

3.2cm(1¼")
── 65cm(25⁹⁄₁₆") (Piece for entire lenght) ──
Batting position

※Cut batting for same size.

(0.8)

4cm(1⁵⁄₈")

Handle
Old rose 1 piece

⊠
no seam allowance
── 13cm(5⅛") ──

b. Cut for corner and turn over from stripe.

④ Bind outer, lining, batting, ③ and sew after basted.

──0.8cm(⁵⁄₁₆")

B

0.8cm(⁵⁄₁₆)

a. Machine stitch

Old rose
(Lining)
(Outer)
Stripe(Outer)

Batting

Outline stitch } Gray
Chain stitch

☆ 2 strands

① Embroider the fabric.

② Bind batting on ① and do an applique.

Outline stitch
Macrame stitch
French knot stitch (2 twists)
Golden yellow
Satin stitch

23.8cm(9⅜")

B

0.8cm(⁵⁄₁₆")

③ Bind bias strip B and batting fold in half and baste.

(0.5cm(³⁄₁₆"))

Embroidely faburic

Old rose
Batting } 1 each

(no seam allowance)

1 cm(⅜")

B

A

⑤ Piping.

3.5cm(1⅜")

(Right side) 1 cm(⅜")

Batting Basted

(Wrong side)
Blind stitch

a. Sew with right sides together.

(Wrong side)

── 1 cm(⅜")

b. Turn back and blind stitch

⑥ Make handle and attach it. Sew with right sides together.

1 cm(⅜")

5.5cm(2³⁄₁₆")

no seam allowance   Piping   A

Kitchen
Shelf lining
Instructions on page 18

Shelf lining
Kitchen
PICTURE ON P.16

Materials (for 1)

- Light olive green soft denim 57cm×34cm
  $(22^7/_{16}"×13^3/_8")$
- Light blue cotton 57cm×34cm
  $(22^7/_{16}"×13^3/_8")$
- #25 embroidery floss moss green, salmon pink

Finished size···55cm×31.5cm$(21^5/_8"×12^3/_8")$

Actual size

☆Use 4 strands

Outline stitch
Moss green

Lazy daisy stitch
Outline stitch } Salmon pink

Finishing line

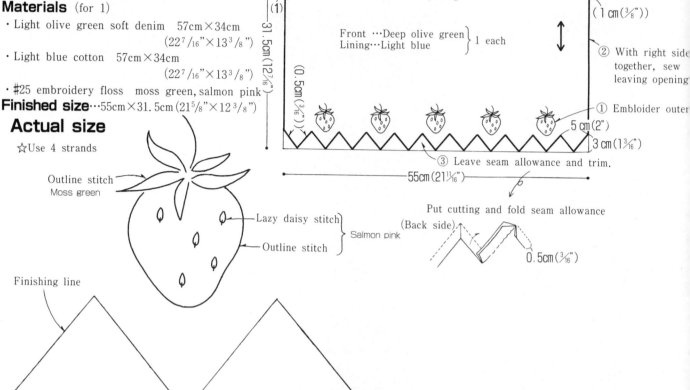

☆ seam allowance indicated in ( )

(1cm($3/_8$"))

④ Turn over and machine stitch.

17cm($6^{11}/_{16}$")
Opening

0.2cm($1/_{16}$")

(1)

31.5cm(12$^7/_8$")

(0.5cm($3/_{16}$"))

Front ···Deep olive green
Lining···Light blue } 1 each

(1cm($3/_8$"))

② With right side together, sew leaving opening

① Embloider outer

5cm(2")

3cm($1^3/_{16}$")

③ Leave seam allowance and trim.

55cm(21$^{11}/_{16}$")

Put cutting and fold seam allowance
(Back side)

0.5cm($3/_{16}$")

Continuing page 35

⟨Coster⟩
Materials (for 1)

- Shirting fabric yellow, grayish green
  12cm($4^3/_4$") square each.
- #25 embroidery floss moss green, beige,
  powder green, chrome yellow

Finished size···10cm(4") square

☆seam alloeance is 1cm($3/_8$")

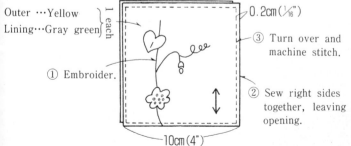

Outer ···Yellow
Lining···Gray green } 1 each

0.2cm($1/_{16}$")

③ Turn over and machine stitch.

① Embroider.

② Sew right sides together, leaving opening.

10cm(4")

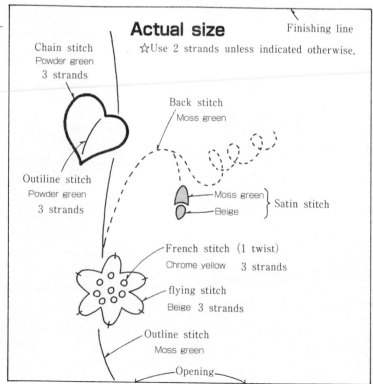

Actual size
Finishing line

☆Use 2 strands unless indicated otherwise.

Chain stitch
Powder green
3 strands

Back stitch
Moss green

Outiline stitch
Powder green
3 strands

Moss green
Beige } Satin stitch

French stitch (1 twist)
Chrome yellow   3 strands

flying stitch
Beige 3 strands

Outline stitch
Moss green

Opening

18

Wall hanging with poket
Living Room

■■
■■
PICTURE ON P.28

Materials
- Blue stripe cotton 33cm×83cm (13"×32$\frac{11}{16}$")
- Light blue stripe cotton 30cm×20cm
  (11$\frac{13}{16}$"×8")
- Light blue cotton 30cm×20cm
  (11$\frac{13}{16}$"×8")
- Batting 30cm×40cm (11$\frac{13}{16}$"×15$\frac{3}{4}$")
- Glue batting 18cm×40cm (7"×11")
- #25 embroidery floss   orient blue,
                drub, coral pink, white

Finished size 30cm×40cm (11$\frac{13}{16}$"×15$\frac{3}{4}$")

Acutal size
Outline stitch 1 strand
unless indicated otherwise

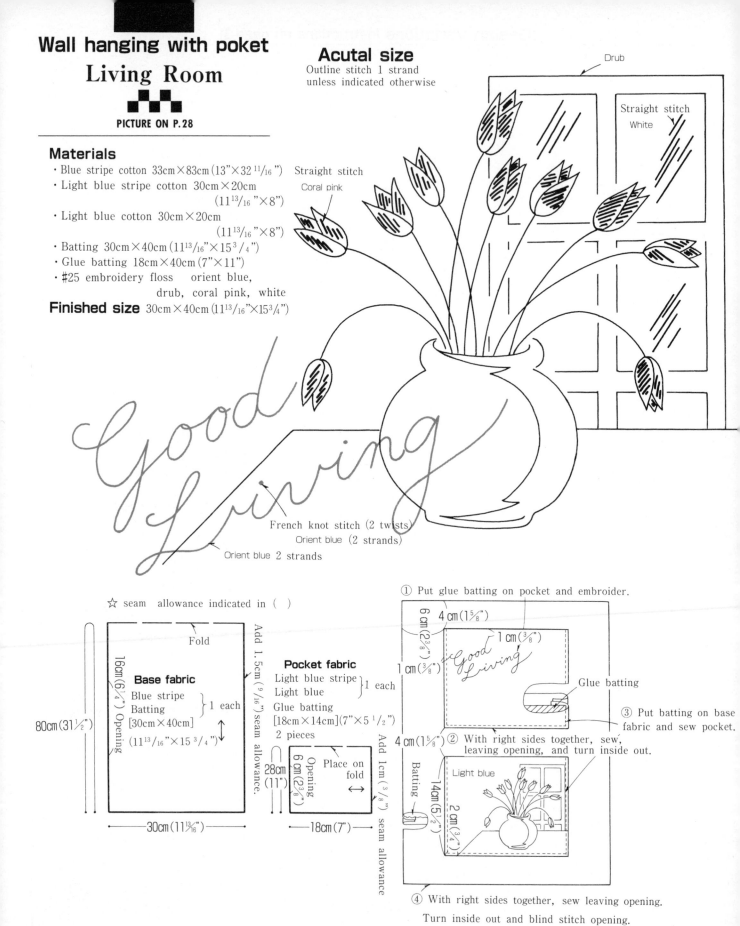

Drub

Straight stitch
White

Straight stitch
Coral pink

French knot stitch (2 twists)
Orient blue (2 strands)

Orient blue 2 strands

☆ seam allowance indicated in ( )

Fold

Add 1.5cm($\frac{9}{16}$") seam allowance.

16cm(6$\frac{1}{4}$") Opening

Base fabric
Blue stripe
Batting } 1 each
[30cm×40cm]
(11$\frac{13}{16}$"×15$\frac{3}{4}$")

80cm(31$\frac{1}{2}$")

30cm(11$\frac{13}{16}$")

Pocket fabric
Light blue stripe } 1 each
Light blue
Glue batting
[18cm×14cm](7"×5$\frac{1}{2}$")
2 pieces

28cm
(11")

Opening
6cm(2$\frac{3}{8}$")

Place on
fold

Add 1cm($\frac{3}{8}$") seam allowance

18cm(7")

① Put glue batting on pocket and embroider.

6cm(2$\frac{3}{8}$")   4cm(1$\frac{5}{8}$")

1cm($\frac{3}{8}$")

1cm($\frac{3}{8}$")

Good Living

Glue batting

③ Put batting on base
fabric and sew pocket.

4cm(1$\frac{5}{8}$") ② With right sides together, sew,
leaving opening, and turn inside out.

Batting

Light blue

14cm(5$\frac{1}{2}$")

2cm($\frac{3}{4}$")

④ With right sides together, sew leaving opening.
Turn inside out and blind stitch opening.

30

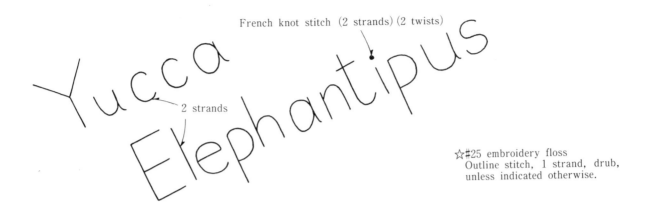

French knot stitch (2 strands) (2 twists)

Yucca

2 strands

Elephantipus

☆#25 embroidery floss
Outline stitch, 1 strand, drub,
unless indicated otherwise.

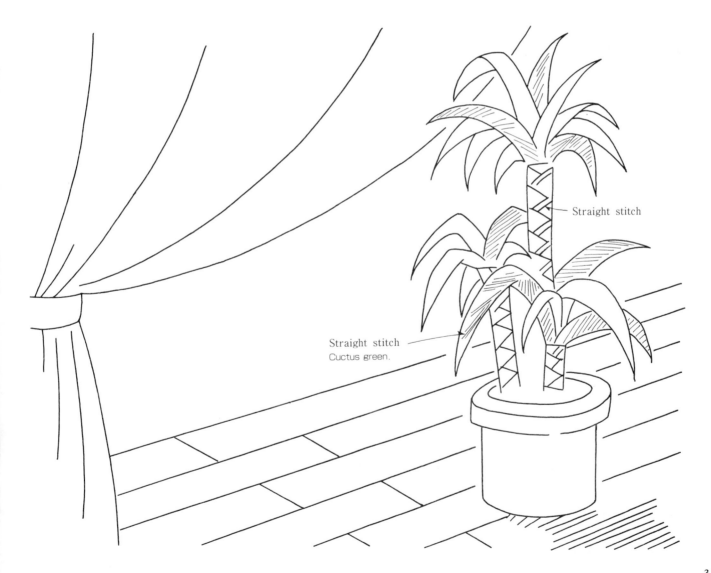

Straight stitch

Straight stitch
Cuctus green.

Dining Room

Table center and Coasters
Instructions on page 34

32

Table center and Coasters
Dining Room

PICTURE ON P.32

⟨Table center⟩
Materials

· Grey green shirting fabric 67cm×41cm

$(26^3/_8"×16^1/_8")$

· #25 embroidery floss beige, carrot red,

motmot green, emerald green, light yellow

Finished size   61cm×35cm $(24"×13^3/_4")$

Actual size

☆ 3 strands unless indicated otherwise.

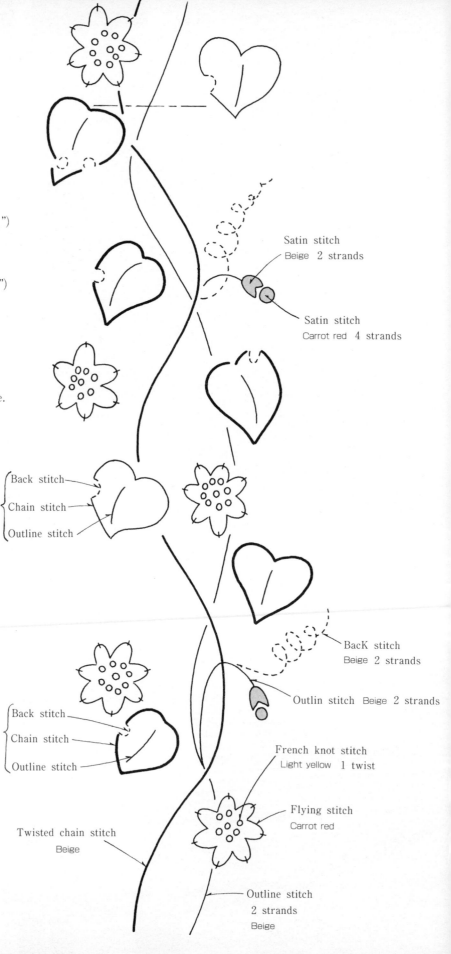

Satin stitch
Beige 2 strands

Satin stitch
Carrot red 4 strands

Emerald green { Back stitch
Chain stitch
Outline stitch

BacK stitch
Beige 2 strands

Outlin stitch Beige 2 strands

French knot stitch
Light yellow 1 twist

Motmot green { Back stitch
Chain stitch
Outline stitch

Flying stitch
Carrot red

Twisted chain stitch
Beige

Outline stitch
2 strands
Beige

Design Variations (Actual size) • page 45

☆#25 embroidery floss, 3 strands,
back stitch, unless indicated otherwise.

Scarlet

Straight stitch

Rose pink

Satin stitch

French knot stitch (1 twist)

Straight stitch

Running stitch

Scarlet

Flying stitch

Straight stitch

Scarlet

Straght stitch

French knot stitch
(1 twist)

Rose pink

Straight stitch

Lazydaisy stitch

Straight stitch

Straight stitch

Satin stitch

Rose pink

Running stitch

Rose pink

French knot stitch (1 twist)

Cross stitch

Running stitch

Straight stitch

Rose pink

Straight stitch

Running stitch

Scarlet

Rose pink

Bath Room

Bath Mat

Instructions on page 50

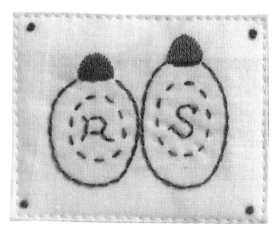

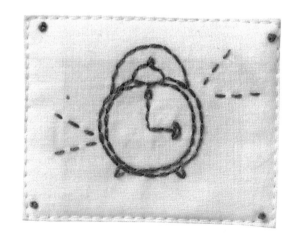

Bath Mat
Bath Room

PICTURE ON P.48

Materials

- Blue check cotton 63cm×53cm (24¹³⁄₁₆"×20⅞")
- Blue towel   55cm ×45cm (21¹¹⁄₁₆"×17¾")
- White cotton   18cm ×15cm (7"×6")
- #25 embroidery floss   queen blue

Finished size   55cm×45cm (21¹¹⁄₁₆"×17¾")

Actual size

☆ 3 strands and back stitch, unless indicated otherwise.

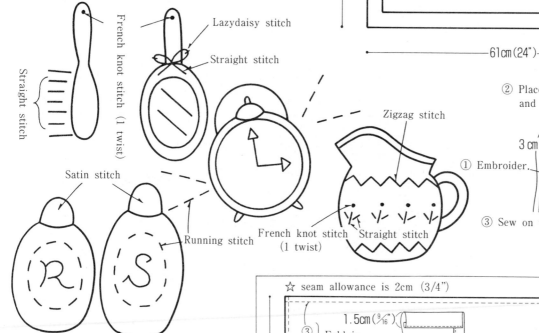

French knot stitch (1 twist)

Straight stitch

Lazydaisy stitch

Straight stitch

Zigzag stitch

Satin stitch

Running stitch

French knot stitch (1 twist)   Straight stitch

☆ seam alloeance is indicated in ( )

55cm (21¹¹⁄₁₆")
(seamis 1cm (⅜"))
3 cm (1³⁄₁₆")
3 cm (1³⁄₁₆")
no seam allowance neeaded
5.5cm (2³⁄₁₆")
Embroidery fabric White 4 pieces
(seam is 1cm (⅜"))
7cm (2¾")
Check fabric 1piece
Towel 1 piece
French knot stitch (2 twists) 3 strands
51cm (20")
45cm (17¼")
61cm (24")

② Place check fabric around towel and fold, a, b and machine stitch.

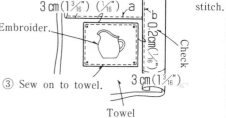

0.2cm (¹⁄₁₆")
3 cm (1³⁄₁₆")
a
④ Blind stitch.
① Embroider.
0.2cm (¹⁄₁₆")
Check
③ Sew on to towel.
3 cm (1³⁄₁₆")
Towel

Continued from page 42

‹Neckline cover for blanket›
Materials

- White cotton 124cm×84cm (49"×33")
- #25 embroidery floss   powder green

Finished size ··· 120cm×80cm (47¼"×31½")

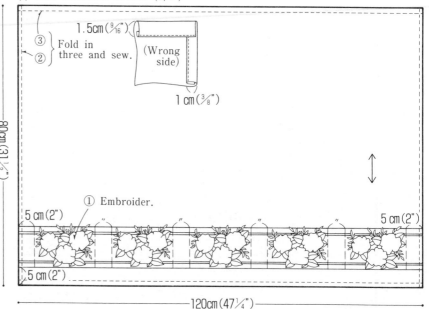

☆ seam allowance is 2cm (3/4")

1.5cm (⁹⁄₁₆")
③ Fold in
② three and sew.
(Wrong side)
1 cm (⅜")
80cm (31½")
① Embroider.
5 cm (2")
5 cm (2")
5 cm (2")
5 cm (2")
120cm (47¼")

Towel stacker
Kitchen

PICTURE ON P.13

Materials

- Printed cotton 90cm (35⁷⁄₁₆") square
- White cotton 90cm×55cm (35⁷⁄₁₆"×21¹¹⁄₁₆")
- Batting 90cm×55cm (35⁷⁄₁₆"×21¹¹⁄₁₆")
- Clear vinyl 8cm×20cm (3¹⁄₈"×7⁷⁄₈")
- 2.5cm (1") wide Velcro 5cm (2")
- #25 embroidery floss　coral pink,
  cherry-bloom, pink, bottele green, seacrest

Finished size　Refrr to illustration

☆ seam allowance is indicated in ( )
No seam allowance needed unless indeicated otherwise.

Outer fabric ···Print
Back fabric ···White } 1 each
Batting

Outer fabric···Print
Back fabric ···White } 1 each
Batting

Place for machine stitch.
6cm(2³⁄₈")　0.6cm(¼")　1.5cm(⁹⁄₁₆")
3cm(1³⁄₁₆")　3cm(1³⁄₁₆")　3.5cm(1³⁄₈")
31cm(12¼")

Lid

19cm(7½")

1.5
1.5cm(⁹⁄₁₆")　0.6cm(¼")
1.5cm(⁹⁄₁₆")　1.5cm(⁹⁄₁₆")
3cm(1³⁄₁₆")
24cm(9½")

Bottom

21cm(8¼")

Embroider fabric

Print
2 pieces
1cm(³⁄₈")
20cm(7⁷⁄₈")
1cm(³⁄₈")
5cm(2")

Bias fabric
A=20cm (7⁷⁄₈") [2 pieces]
B=24cm (9½") [1 pieces]

4cm(1⁵⁄₈")　Print　✕

C=80cm (31½") [1 piece]
D, E=90cm (35½") [1 piece each]

Satin stitch Coral pink
Satin stitch Bottle green
Satin stitch Seacrest

Place to attach embroidered fabric.
3cm(1³⁄₁₆")　3cm(1³⁄₁₆")　3cm(1³⁄₁₆")　2cm(¾")
20cm(7⁷⁄₈")
5cm(⁹⁄₁₆")　7.5cm(3")　2cm(¾")

1.5cm(⁹⁄₁₆")　3cm(1³⁄₁₆")　3　3　2cm(¾")

Side section

Place to put velcro.

Opening 1.5cm(⁹⁄₁₆")　0.7cm(⁵⁄₁₆")　21cm
3cm(1³⁄₁₆")　1.5cm(⁹⁄₁₆")　(8¼")　23cm(9¹⁄₁₆")
19cm(7½")　2cm(¾")　7.5cm(3")　1.5cm(⁹⁄₁₆")

Vinyl 1 piece
(1cm(³⁄₈"))
6cm(2³⁄₈")

82cm(32¼")

Actual size
2 strands

⑩ Put velcro.
1.5cm(⁹⁄₁₆")
⑦ Turn inside out of front section, lid, and add piping.
1cm(³⁄₈")
⑨ Machine stitch 4 edges (pick little bit).
① Bind outer, back fabric and batting and machine stitch.

⑥ Piping except for lid●make place.

③ Appliqué embroider fabric on side section.

20cm(7⁷⁄₈")　Vinyl　①

④ Sew viny.　21cm(8¼")

D
C
A
1cm(³⁄₈")
B
E
23cm(9¹⁄₁₆")　①

⑧ Turn bottom and side section inside out and add piping.

⑤ Use bias fabric for piping.

② Embroider on fabric.

Outer fabric (Right side)
Bias fabric A
ack fabric ong side)
Vinyl　1cm(³⁄₈")
Batting

a. Sew with right sides together.
b. Fold back side, attach vinyl and machine stitch.

Back fabric (Right side)
1cm(³⁄₈")

a. Sew with right sides together.
b. Fold to back and blindstitch.

Coral pink
Cherry-bloom
Pink

Long and short stitch

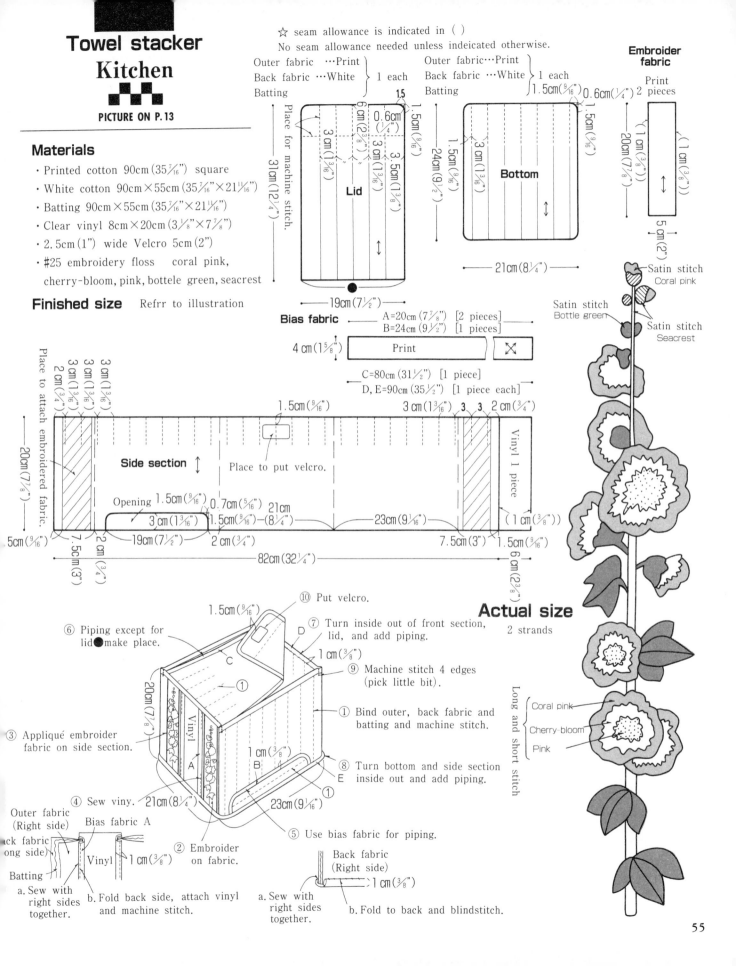

55

Family Room

Miniature Frame
Instructions on page 58

Miniture Frame
Family Room

PICTURE ON P.56

Materials

· White cotton 18cm (7") square
· Artificial wood frame, inside diameter 13cm (5⅛")
· #25 embroidery floss   shadow green, pea green, spring green, dark blue green, ochre orange, pink, crimson, blue purple, black, viridian green

Finished sise   Same as frame

Instructions   Cut embroidery fabric 18cm (7 1/16") diameter, gathering stitched around and put it into frame.

Actual size

☆ 2 strands unless indicated otherwise

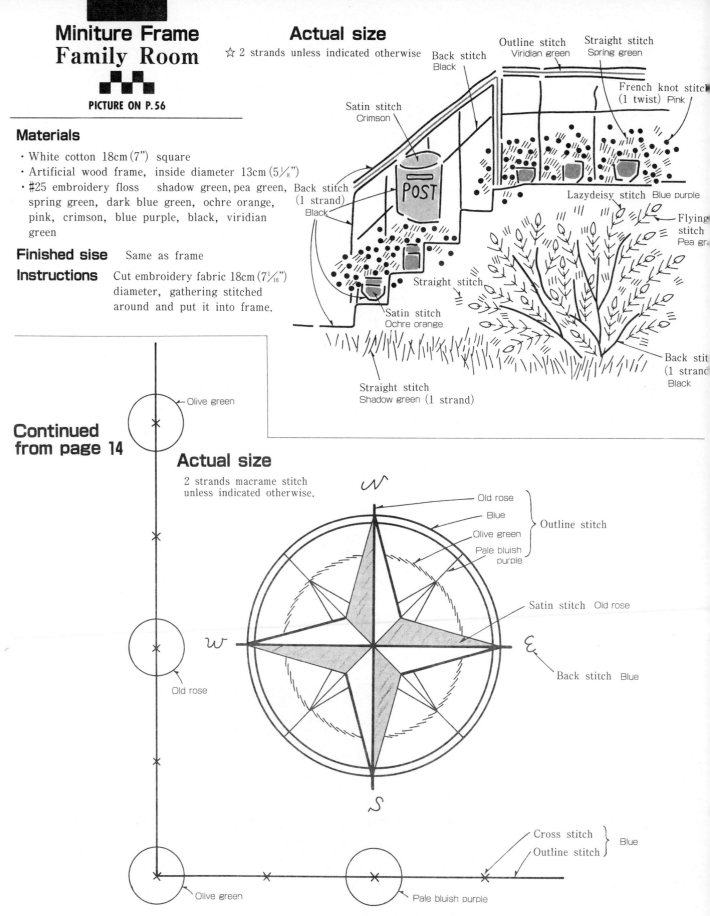

Outline stitch
Viridian green

Straight stitch
Spring green

Back stitch
Black

Satin stitch
Crimson

French knot stitch
(1 twist) Pink

Back stitch
(1 strand)
Black

Lazydeisy stitch Blue purple

Flying stitch
Pea green

Straight stitch

Satin stitch
Ochre orange

Back stitch
(1 strand)
Black

Straight stitch
Shadow green (1 strand)

Continued
from page 14

Olive green

Actual size

2 strands macrame stitch unless indicated otherwise.

Old rose
Blue
Olive green
Pale bluish purple

Outline stitch

Satin stitch Old rose

Back stitch Blue

Old rose

Cross stitch
Outline stitch
Blue

Olive green

Pale bluish purple

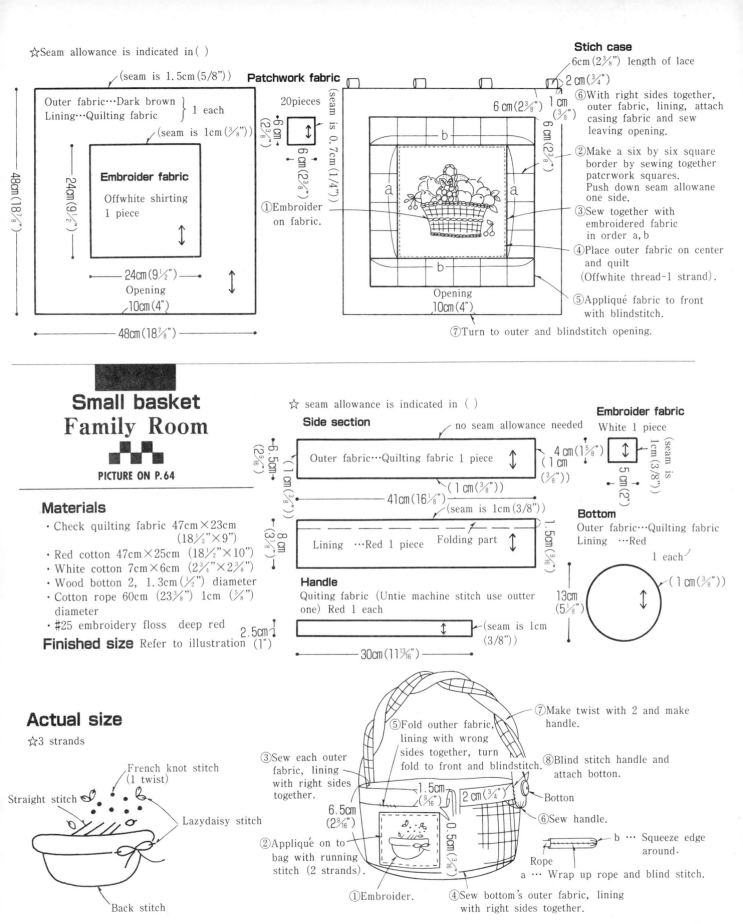

☆Seam allowance is indicated in ( )

(seam is 1.5cm (5/8"))

Outer fabric···Dark brown ⎫
Lining···Quilting fabric ⎭ 1 each

(seam is 1cm (3/8"))

48cm (18⅞")

24cm (9½")

Embroider fabric

Offwhite shirting
1 piece

24cm (9½")

Opening
10cm (4")

48cm (18⅞")

Patchwork fabric

20pieces

(seam is 0.7cm (1/4"))

6cm (2⅜")

6cm (2⅜")

①Embroider
on fabric.

Stich case

6cm (2⅜") length of lace

2 cm (¾")

6 cm (2⅜")

1 cm (3/8")

6 cm (2⅜")

b

a   a

b

Opening
10cm (4")

⑥With right sides together,
outer fabric, lining, attach
casing fabric and sew
leaving opening.

②Make a six by six square
border by sewing together
patcrwork squares.
Push down seam allowane
one side.

③Sew together with
embroidered fabric
in order a, b

④Place outer fabric on center
and quilt
(Offwhite thread-1 strand).

⑤Appliqué fabric to front
with blindstitch.

⑦Turn to outer and blindstitch opening.

Small basket
Family Room

PICTURE ON P.64

Materials

· Check quilting fabric 47cm×23cm
  (18½"×9")
· Red cotton 47cm×25cm (18½"×10")
· White cotton 7cm×6cm (2¾"×2⅜")
· Wood botton 2, 1.3cm (½") diameter
· Cotton rope 60cm (23⅜") 1cm (⅝")
  diameter
· #25 embroidery floss deep red

Finished size Refer to illustration

☆ seam allowance is indicated in ( )

Side section

no seam allowance needed

Outer fabric···Quilting fabric 1 piece

6.5cm (2⁹⁄₁₆")

1 cm (3/8")

4 cm (1⅝")
(1 cm (3/8"))

41cm (16⅛")

(1 cm (3/8"))

(seam is 1cm (3/8"))

8cm (3⅛")

Lining ···Red 1 piece   Folding part

1.5cm (⁹⁄₁₆")

Embroider fabric

White 1 piece

4 cm (1⅝")

5 cm (2")

(seam is 1cm (3/8"))

Bottom

Outer fabric···Quilting fabric
Lining ···Red

1 each

(1 cm (3/8"))

13cm (5⅛")

Handle

Quiting fabric (Untie machine stitch use outter
one) Red 1 each

2.5cm (1")

30cm (11¹³⁄₁₆")

(seam is 1cm (3/8"))

Actual size

☆3 strands

French knot stitch
(1 twist)

Straight stitch

Lazydaisy stitch

Back stitch

⑤Fold outher fabric,
lining with wrong
sides together, turn
fold to front and blindstitch.

③Sew each outer
fabric, lining
with right sides
together.

1.5cm (⁹⁄₁₆")

6.5cm (2⁹⁄₁₆")

2 cm (¾")

0.5cm (³⁄₁₆")

②Appliqué on to
bag with running
stitch (2 strands).

①Embroider.

④Sew bottom's outer fabric, lining
with right sides together.

⑦Make twist with 2 and make
handle.

⑧Blind stitch handle and
attach botton.

Botton

⑥Sew handle.

b ··· Squeeze edge
around·

Rope

a ··· Wrap up rope and blind stitch.

Family Room

Small basket

Instructions on page 63